Wings

Michele L. Smith

Wings

Scripture quotations in this publication are taken from the King James Version unless otherwise noted. Copyright info for all versions used in this book are listed on the References page.

ISBN 978-0-692-94983-2

Cover Design and Interior Layout Design by Donna Osborn Clark at www.CreationByDonna.com

Published by Royal Word Publications
All Rights Reserved
Printed in the United States of America

Address inquiries to:
Michele Smith
404 E. 1st Street
Unit 1445
Long Beach, CA 90802

This book is dedicated to my grandchildren Alijah, Aliyah and Brielle, who are the best grandkids a grandmother could ask for: happy, loving and a joy to be with. I love spending time with you and it's a blessing watching you grow. Always know Nana loves you more.

Acknowledgments

To Terri and Tammy,

For your love and support, thank you for pushing me out of my comfort zone. I am so excited in anticipation of all that is coming our way as we launch iCelebrateHER. Cheers to you for all that you are and all you do!

To Donna,

Once again you have come through in grand style! You pressed through to be here for me in spite of all you are enduring and I am grateful. I pray God continue to bless the work of your hands and prosper you in every area of your life.

Table of Contents

"Poetry is when emotion has found its thought and the thought has found words..." **Robert Frost**

A Place in My Heart

"My command is this: Love each other as I have loved you. Greater love has no one than this: to lay down one's life for one's friends."
John 15:12-13 (NIV)

Since the first day we met, right from the very start,
You captured a very special place,
In the deepest part of my heart.
From a walk in the park, to hours on the phone,
An unbreakable bond between us has grown.
A treasure of priceless jewels,
Is what I've found in you.
Diamonds and pearls though beautiful and rare,
Can't even come close or remotely compare,
To the love and friendship, we've come to share.
A smile, a hug or a tender touch
Simple ways you've shown that you care so much.
We've talked, we've laughed, we've even cried.
We've shared some incredible, unforgettable times.
Though we don't know
What the future holds in store,
I am certain my life is truly better than before.
I thank you for all you have been to me,
For loving and accepting me unconditionally.
I am encouraged by your dreams, I believe in you.
I pray that you keep climbing
Until your dreams come true.
And on those dark days when I'm down and blue
I'll close my eyes and think of you.
Because even when we are far apart,
You're always there
In the deepest part of my heart!

A Grain of Faith

He replied, "Because you have so little faith. Truly I tell you, if you have faith as small as a mustard seed, you can say to this mountain, 'Move from here to there,' and it will move. Nothing will be impossible for you." Matthew 17:20

I am mustard seed, small I am, small indeed,
Created He me and named me mustard seed.
I am praying for you, interceding daily,
That you can begin with me to trust and believe.
That you learn to understand me,
The mustard seed
Because I have no limbs to walk,
Nor eyes to see,
And when planted,
I will not become the tallest tree.
Yet I represent all that God asks of you,
To have faith and believe that He is real and true.
When you look at me what do you see?
I pray you see the reflection of the Father's beauty,
Yes, in something as small and insignificant as me.
God abounds powerful and oh so mighty,
If you can manage to muster faith as large as me.
Nothing is impossible,
Blessings will flow bountifully.
Faith is the foundation of life and salvation,
Without faith life is hopeless and full of destruction.
Keep me close, keep His word near,
Pray
your prayers in faith,
And God will always hear.
The life that you are seeking begins here with me,
Faith as a grain of mustard seed.

Michele L. Smith

Everything that seek will surely be yours
When you let go and let God
When you...Truly BELIEVE!

A Life of Peace

*Do not be anxious about anything, but in every situation, by prayer
and petition, with thanksgiving, present your requests to God.[7] And
the peace of God, which transcends all understanding, will guard your
hearts and your minds in Christ Jesus.* Philippians 4:6-7 (NIV)

Noah built the ark
Joshua dreamed the dreams
The children of Israel walked the desert
The Hebrew boys were tried in the fire
The disciples left everything they owned
All to pave the way
For a Life of Peace
Moses parted the red sea
Jesus took a beating on the road to Calvary
Then He hung and died for you and me
All to pave the way
For a Life of Peace
God's prophets have spoken
His promises shall not be broken
God's will is that you have life
And have it more abundantly
That you would fulfill purpose and walk in destiny
That your days would be happy
That you dwell in tranquility
Living
Always
A Life of Peace!

Michele L. Smith

"The only person you are destined to become is the person you decide to be." **Ralph Waldo Emerson**

Bag Lady

*but let your adorning be the hidden person of the heart with the
imperishable beauty of a gentle and quiet spirit, which in God's sight
is very precious.* I Peter 3:4 (ESV)

You were not created to carry the load
To bear this life's burdens all on your own
I made you in my image, after my own heart
With hopes that from me you would never depart.
As you ventured out and went your own way
Life as you knew it got harder each day.
You started out with one bag, then two or three
Now you're surrounded with bags a plenty.
And it pains my heart like you would not believe
Because I never meant for you to be a Bag Lady.
You've stored so many things in all of those bags
So many feelings and hang-ups
You'd never have enough tags
To identify all the junk you're holding on to
I sit here silently watching, waiting for you.
You weigh yourself down
Carrying those bags all over town
So many times when you arrive
Your lovely smile turned into a frown.
The weight gets so heavy
Sometimes it makes you cry
I wish you understood my child
I never meant for you to be a Bag Lady.
Sometimes you'll empty a bag
You'll even throw it away
This is a good time – you feel happy this day.
This is a day of accomplishment

You are proud of yourself – it was time well spent.
Bags were created as a help aid only
To temporarily hold things
Make them easier to carry
They were not designed as storage bins
In which to allow your emotions to toil and tarry.
Precious and rare you are to me
Never did I mean you to be a Bag Lady.
Yes, I know some of the bags are oh so pretty
You say to yourself, "this is one I wanna keep."
But please remember daughter – you are not a Bag Lady.
You are more precious to me than silver and gold
My heart fills with joy
Each time your testimony is told
Told to another sister hurting and in need
To strengthen and encourage her
Keep her from becoming a Bag Lady.
Destroy all the baggage
Causing you sadness and strife
 My goal is that you have life
And life abundantly
Not life that fits into a bag
You are not a Bag Lady.
You are special to me beyond your wildest dreams
A bag my dear child
Could never hold all that I have for you.
Trust me and believe…I declare it is true
I am your Father and I Love You!
Empty the bags and in me take rest
Reach out and claim your treasure chest
The treasure chest
That holds everything that you need
Because you are not a Bag Lady,
But a woman of Purpose, Integrity, Destiny and Royalty!

Because

The LORD hath appeared of old unto me, [saying], Yea, I have loved thee with an everlasting love: therefore with loving kindness have I drawn thee. Jeremiah 31:3

When others said I would amount to nothing
When I feel inside as though I'm self-destructing
When evil's darkness clouds my sky
When in the pain of midnight I question why
You've whispered strength into my desperate ear
Taught me you'd talk to me, if I'm inclined to hear
Encouraged me to confront and conquer my fears
You've wiped away burning and raging tears
So that each day me eyes open I can face the world
Rise above the earthly chaos, drama and turmoil
As I learn to wade the waters of the storm
Recognizing there's no weapon
That can bring me harm
That with you on my side I can handle anything
Because…
Totally
Completely
Unconditionally
You love me.

When my flesh succumbs as it is weak
When my lips can't form the right words to speak
When obstacles surface and I'm sure I'll fail
When my hopes and dreams seem
They won't prevail
With mustard seed faith
I slip my hands in your hands

You empower me with endurance to stand
For your Word declares I need only believe
And walking in faith releases the grace I receive
Grace that says I'm a child of the most-high king
That my Father shall supply all my needs
That with you on my side I can do anything
Because
Totally
Completely
Unconditionally…You Love Me!

Deliver Me

And call upon me in the day of trouble: I will deliver thee, and thou shalt glorify me. Psalm 50:15

Deliver me O Lord from the heartache and pain
Deliver me O Lord from the guilt and the shame
Deliver me O Lord from the darkness of night
Deliver me O Lord into the glorious light

Deliver me O Lord from greed and selfishness
Deliver me O Lord to a place of holiness
Deliver me O Lord from all that's negative
Deliver me O Lord each day you bless me to live

Deliver me O Lord from the pits of hell
Deliver me O Lord for I have a story to tell
Deliver me O Lord from insecurity
Deliver me O Lord to be a sanctuary

Deliver me O Lord from unforgiveness
Deliver me O Lord to a place of faithfulness
Deliver me O Lord that I might not sin against thee
Deliver me O Lord to help set the captives free

Deliver me O Lord from bondage
Deliver me O Lord from the wicked men's faces
Deliver me O Lord so that my life shows no traces
Shows no traces of things that are not of you
But rather shows others
I'm alive today only because of you

Deliver me O Lord from the spirit of fear
Deliver me O Lord
That your voice is the only one I hear
Deliver me O Lord to truth and righteousness
Deliver me O Lord
So that other lives may be blessed
Thank you O Lord for Delivering me and Setting me FREE!

"Following Christ is not a casual or occasional practice but a continuous way of life that applies at all times and in all places."
Elder Dallin H. Oaks

Following God's Lead

Lead me in thy truth, and teach me: for thou art the God of my salva-
tion; on thee do I wait all the day. Psalm 25:5

I have a vision, I have a dream
I'm filled with so much excitement
I feel like I could scream
Scream about God's goodness
His mercy and grace
Reflecting on how he's caring for me
As I run this Christian race
The race to reach the souls that are lost
Recognizing His sacrificial blessing
As he paid the ultimate cost
Sacrificing himself for me to have a chance
A chance at a life so amazing
Rising above and beyond any circumstance
I'm living for a purpose
I've got a mission to fulfill
Even on the long and dreary days
When the road of life seems all up hill
I must press on, I cannot quit
Because life as I once knew it no longer exists
God is in control, He is paving the path
Providing instruction and guidance
For my appointed tasks
There's much for me to gain
And just as much to learn
And all I merely need to do
Is turn to God and ask
Ask Him all the questions
Take them all to him in prayer

Wings

Knowing that he's leading me
And that he's always there
When I stumble I only need
To fall down on my knees
For faith steps in to remind me again
There's just one lesson to heed
That everything in life is manageable
As long as I'm Following God's lead.

Gift of Grace

*For by grace are ye saved through faith; and that not of yourselves: it
is the gift of God:* Ephesians 2:8

The smiles you put on a child's face,
Are proof that God has blessed you,
With the gift of grace.
To handle the challenges the children have faced,
To teach them how to walk in faith.
Your home is one of safety and refuge,
For those who have suffered all kinds of abuse.
They will come and they will go,
There will be times when they will not know.
How to express the feelings deep inside,
Or the reasons they long to run away and hide.
Yet God will guide you in how to meet their needs,
As long as His will you continue to heed.
He'll meet every need and give so much more,
For you there are double portion blessings in store.
Times may get hard and your patience runs thin,
Stand strong and remember you must never give in.
In the dark of the storm, at the midnight hour,
Remember through His Word
You have all the power.
When the money seems short and times seem hard,
Remember to thank and praise the Lord.
For through it all He continues to make a way,
Joy will fill your soul with each passing day.
Bask in His glory; boldly share your story,
For someone's salvation hinges on your testimony.
Remember the smiles on the face of a child,
Be encouraged...believing it's all been worthwhile.

For the rest of your days,
As you continue running the race,
Praise God for blessing you with
The Gift of Grace!

God's Love – God's Grace

*for all have sinned and fall short of the glory of God, and all are
justified freely by his grace through the redemption that came by
Christ Jesus.* Romans 3:23-24 (NIV)

Skies that scatter shades of the rainbow,
Oceans that pour out in glorious waves of blues,
The rising of the sun and blowing of the wind,
Signs and wonders of God's great love for you.

Trees that climb to meet the sky,
The simple smile on a young child's face,
Mountains that scale across the earth,
Signs and wonders of God's most awesome grace.

Rain drops that fall and shower the land,
Flowers in sunlight topped with morning dew,
Good deeds done by those who take a stand,
Sings and wonders of God's great love for you.

Sparrows that fly and robins that sing,
Unity in spirit spreading from place to place,
Bodies healed, prophecies revealed,
Signs and wonders of God's most awesome grace.

Conquering fears that had you in bondage,
People that encourage and don't even know you,
Gifts and talents and a free will to choose,
Signs and wonders of God's great love for you.

Wings

Relief from sorrow and ongoing forgiveness
Joy and mercy renewed each day,
Correction and deliverance from selfishness,
Signs and wonders of God's most awesome grace.

All that's required is that you believe,
Give only in love and love you'll receive,
Confess in His name and set yourself free,
Trust Him to supply all of your needs.

Freedom is yours to pray praise and sing,
Come just as you are and all your faults bring,
With faith in your heart and peace in your mind,
God's love and God's grace are yours at all times.

"Peace. It does not mean to be in a place where there is no noise, trouble or hard work. It means to be in the midst of all those things and be calm in your heart." **Unknown**

His Peace Abides

Thou wilt keep him in perfect peace, whose mind is stayed on thee:
because he trusteth in thee. Isaiah 26:3

In the darkest hour of the darkest day,
Don't be sad there's no need to cry.
Lift your voice in praise,
God's peace abides.
When everything in your life,
Seems to crash and collide,
Just call on Jesus
Because
God's peace abides,
His peace abides in those who believe,
His peace abides when you're open to receive.
Reach down inside,
God's peace abides,
In your spirit!

I Thank God Today

In everything give thanks: for this is the will of God in Christ Jesus concerning you. I Thessalonians 5:18

Even when I was blind and did not believe,
Through the stars, the sun and the air that I breathe,
He reminded me of the endless possibilities.
For His mercy and faithfulness,
I thank God today.

Even when I turned my back and took the broad road,
He continued to walk with me balancing out my load,
Even when I disobeyed,
He know someday I'd find my way,
For His mercy and faithfulness,
I thank God today.

Even when I was selfish walking in my flesh,
He refused to let me drown in the stink of my own mess.
Even when all my great plans failed,
He silently whispered in my ear,
"Your ship will still sail!"
For His mercy and faithfulness,
I thank God today.

In spite of weed smoking,
Drinking and negative thinking,
In spite of fornication, gossiping and adultery.

In spite of anger, rebellion and unforgiveness,
In spite of fear, doubt and anxiety,
In spite of secrets, lies and mismanaging financially,

Wings

He continued to have angels watching out for me.
For His mercy and faithfulness,
I thank God today.

In spite of all the things I've done,
He daily reminds me that in Him I have a home.
Every time I fall or go astray,
He lays out the breadcrumbs for me to find my way,
My way back to Him,
And His unconditional love for me.

The love that's better than money and material things,
The love that surpasses all human understanding,
The love that says, "no matter what my child
I'm here for you and here for you I'll stay."
For His mercy and his faithfulness,
I thank God today.

I thank Him that with each passing day
I'm learning to live
Not by my will
But
According to God's way,
For His mercy and his faithfulness
I thank God today!

Lean on Me

Trust in the Lord with all thine heart; and lean not unto thine own understanding. In all thy ways acknowledge him, and he shall direct thy paths. Proverbs 3:5-6

When you are lost and feeling alone,
When your hope is fading and love is gone,
Lean on Me.
When everything seems out of control,
Life's burdens and trials are taking their toll,
Lean on Me.
When times are hard and your bills are due,
When you don't have a clue,
As to what you should do
Lean on Me.
When you think you've got it all figured out
Then fear creeps in and you begin to doubt,
Lean on Me.
When everyone around you has turned away,
When anger and hurt make you feel betrayed,
Lean on Me.
When the man has stopped calling,
When the tears won't stop falling,
Lean on Me.
When life seems a mess,
When you can't control selfishness,
Lean on Me.
When your children rebel,
When everything seems a living hell,
Lean on Me.
When and only when you lean on me
Will your eyes be opened

And you'll be able to see,
That nothing and no one can ever make you free.
But freedom comes from trusting
And believing in me.
I am your Father and I love you so much.
All you need to do is ask for my touch.
I am with you always,
Especially on your darkest day.
If you would only let go and Lean on Me.
Strength for your journey is hidden in my Word,
It's the weapon to fight all your battles,
It's your heavenly sword.
Love and encouragement to you I freely give,
Each and every day of this life you live.
So, when you are ready to give me some time,
Cry out to me and I'll be there,
Because my desire for you is that you never despair.
Free yourself of all the frustration and pain.
Free yourself from the guilt and shame.
Free yourself from bitterness and strife.
Free yourself form all the negative ties.
Free yourself to rest in me.
Let go and allow me to set you free.
Let go of it all, Lean on Me and be FREE!
I love you my child, I love you indeed.

Michele L. Smith

"Faith expects from God what is beyond all expectation."

Andrew Murray

Let Us Be Thankful

And say ye, Save us, O God of our salvation, and gather us together, and deliver us from the heathen, that we may give thanks to thy holy name, and glory in thy praise. I Chronicles 16:35

Let us give thanks to God above
Thanks for His mercy and enduring love
Seen in the waves of the oceans and grains of sand
Seen in the valleys and mountains across the land

It is said if you listen to the winds and the trees
In the still of the silence you will hear him speak
Speak of the love for you held in His heart
Speak of the knowledge His word imparts

In the songs of the songbirds His love melody rings
Sweet lyrics of joy His forgiveness brings
Let us be thankful for every living thing
Thankful we to can lift our voices to sing

Let us be thankful for all this life beholds
Thankful that in our lives God unfolds the rose
Lessons we learn that bring us good
Thankful His word is yet by us understood

Let us be thankful for all we are taught
For with His life the price of our sins was bought
Let us be thankful for love and peace
For His sacrifice, we have freedom and liberty

Thankful for the times we were sad and cried
Thankful for those tears one day on the cross He died

Michele L. Smith

Let us be thankful for the rain and the storm
For through it all He shields us from harm

Let us be thankful for the blood that He shed
Thank for the crown of thorns worn on His head
Let us be thankful for every lash and His pain
For because of it we now live freely without shame
Let us be thankful we make it from day to day somehow
Thankful for wonderful lives, right here...right now
Confidently knowing in Him our faith is growing
Assured of salvation for simply confessing and believing

Glory to God, Praise His Almighty name
Thankful for deliverance
And the life from whence we came
Let us be thankful and worry no more
For in Him we have
Great blessings in store
Let us be thankful
Thankful,
Forever more!

Like Never Before

Behold, I will do a new thing; now it shall spring forth; shall ye not know it? I will even make a way in the wilderness, and rivers in the desert. Isaiah 43:19

It's a new season, it's a new day
God is restoring family today in a mighty way.
Roaring like waves of the ocean along the sea shore,
God's spirit is freely flowing today
Like Never Before.
You've seen some good times, you've been blessed,
God is waiting to see if you'll pass the test.
It's not a faith test,
It's a LOVE test.
God wants you to walk in His love
Like Never Before.
You see it's God's love that is His greatest command,
Without love you cannot and will not be able to stand.
The tests and trials that come your way
Will knock you down and cause your whole world to shake.
God says it's time my sons and daughters
For you to get the revelation,
Time that you heed His command,
Time to get in position.
Are you ready children of God?
Are you ready children of God to stand on my word?
Are you ready to obey and follow me Like Never Before?
Are you ready to let go and let God Like Never Before?
Are you ready children of God to receive His joy
Joy…unspeakable joy Like Never Before?
Are you ready children of God to walk in His anointing?
Are you ready children of God to walk in your authority?

Are you ready children of God to walk in prosperity?
Are you ready children of God to let go of envy and jealousy?
Are you ready children of God to be blessed to be a blessing?
Are you ready to stop being busy bodies and gossiping?
Are you ready children of God to do what matters most to me?
Are you ready children of God to follow me Like Never Before?
Some of you need to go back and reconcile with your family.
It's time God says, "To do what matters to me,
It's time to start showing love,
Stop backbiting and gossiping.
Children of God I have called you each by name,
I have forgiven your sins and released all your shame.
I have loved you like nobody can,
I'm waiting for you to slip your hand in my hand.
To live your life according to my will and my appointed plan.
I'm waiting to see if you'll keep the vows you've made to me,
I'm waiting to see if you will help lead the blind to see.
Some of you have forgotten you were once blind yourself,
I brought you out, lifted you up,
Yet you leave your testimony sitting like an old book on a shelf.
I created you for destiny, purpose and for my glory,
Not for you to do as you will,
To be self-centered and self-serving.
My commandment to love is not up for debate,
The time is NOW there's no more time to waste.
I'm calling you this day to stand and come forth,
I'm calling you this day Like Never Before.
Every time you have needed me I've been here for you,
Yet you turn away from my will and do what you want to do,
Expecting me still to keep on blessing you.
I've given you assignments,
And those tasks are left undone,
With no justification for your procrastination,
And still my children are struggling,
Drowning in self-destruction and devastation.

Wings

Their lives are a mess like yours once was,
You turn up your nose,
Your face wears a frown,
You look down on others like you're so holier than thou.
It's a new season, it's a new day,
I'm ready to restore you in a might way,
I'm ready to release my glory Like Never Before.
I love you so much I gave my only Son,
That your life would be a joy-filled and prosperous one.
I'm ready to pour down my anointing Like Never Before.
I'm ready to release my power Like Never Before.
I'm ready to release my peace Like Never Before.
I'm ready to release prosperity Like Never Before.
Spread my love Like Never Before.
It's time children of God to step into the new,
Looking back no more,
Spread my love Like Never Before.

Wings

"but those who hope in the Lord will renew their strength. They will soar on wings like eagles; they will run and not grow weary, they will walk and not be faint." Isaiah 40:31 (NIV)

On the wings of your love is how I fly
Soaring above the earth as an eagle in the sky
Your beauty surrounds my fragile flight
Whispers of the wind are my travel guide
Some days I travel the entire world
Without ever leaving the ground
Some days I'm climbing high to meet the clouds
Some days I hear your voice so clear, so loud
Some days in the stillness you don't utter a sound
Yet you speak to me in ways I can't explain
Just a touch from you erases all the pain
The very life of you exists in me
With every move I make, every breath I breathe
Peace abounds in my battlefield
When I spread my wings and just believe
Flying into purpose and destiny
What a blessed and joy filled journey
As I float on faith and release my mind
On the wings of your love is how I fly!

"My unknown future is in the hands of an all-knowing God."
Unknown

Never Too Busy

And the Lord, he it is that doth go before thee; he will be with thee, he
will not fail thee, neither forsake thee: fear not, neither be dismayed.
Deuteronomy 31:8

There's no limit to my contacting you
In all your work, you let me know I'm important too
You're always there with an attentive ear
Everything I need to say you're willing to hear
The line is always open, the call is always free
Night or day, no matter the time,
You're always there for me
There's never an answering machine
Never a recording or never-ending ring
At a moment's notice to you I'm instantly connected
I never get a wrong number,
My fingers ever re-directed
For me and my life issues you always make the time
You give faster service than the fastest express line
Daily without fail you yearn to hear from me
And even when I think I am—
You are Never Too Busy
Forever faithful and merciful toward me
Just hearing your voice calms me with great peace
And even when I fail to fall on my knees
Fail to give you thanks
Fail to give my love
Fail to make my daily call
You still lift me and help me to stand tall
Still blessing me with the greatest sacrifice of all
Even way back when as you prepared
To bury your own son

Wings

You took the time to stop and consider me
Wanted to assure me that you are Never Too Busy
Never Too Busy to listen and hear me out
Never Too Busy to ease my fears, erase my doubt
Never Too Busy to look out and provide for me
Never Too Busy to grant me your peace
Never Too Busy to put a smile on my face
Never Too Bust to help me grow in my faith
Never Too Busy to guide me in your way
Never Too Busy even when I have gone astray
Never Too Busy to grant me new mercies
Thank you, my Lord for NEVER being Too busy for me!

No Matter What

*And we know that all things work together for good to them that love
God, to them who are the called according to his purpose.*
Romans 8:28

No matter what happens tomorrow
God has it all under control
It is his great pleasure
That you have peace in your soul
No matter what
May come your way
Don't fret, don't be dismayed
So long as you keep your hand in his hand
And
Let him guide you every step of the way....
EVERYTHING
Is going to be OKAY!
For all things work for your good
When you love the Lord.
The joy of the Lord be your strength
Trust him no matter what
Because for you he'll go to the deepest depth
And the longest length
He'll move mountains
He'll calm the raging seas
To ensure that you are
Walking in Confident Peace
Your heart's desire is important to him
Talk to him
He'll talk back
For you he's always ready to listen
For he loves you more than you can imagine
He loves you...No Matter What!

Remember When

*though its waters roar and foam and the mountains quake with their
surging.⁴ There is a river whose streams make glad the city of God, the
holy place where the Most High dwells.⁵ God is within her, she will
not fall; God will help her at break of day.⁶ Nations are in uproar,
kingdoms fall; he lifts his voice, the earth melts.⁷ The Lord Almighty is
with us; the God of Jacob is our fortress.* Psalm 46:3-7 (NIV)

Remember when you felt so afraid
When someone left you felt should have stayed
Remember when couldn't sleep at night
When you wanted someone there to hold you tight

Remember when your body ached
From your head to your toes
When you cried out for someone
To listen to your woes
Remember when to me you turned your back
When you were only interested
 In getting high on crack

Remember when you tried to drown your thoughts,
You didn't want to think
When all you cared about each day
Was having another drink

Remember when you slit your wrists,
Tried to commit suicide
When you woke up the next morning
Wondering why you had not died

Remember when you were abused
And had not the courage to leave
Remember when you challenged me

Michele L. Smith

Because you did not believe
When you cursed me
Because you felt I gave you no reprieve

It is often easy to stay hung up on the past
But my prayer is that you recognize
That the storms of life don't last
I pray that you remember
When you wake each day with breath
Remember that I've paved the way
For you to stand every test

Remember when
I bore the cross and wore the crown of thorns
Remember that I did this before you were even born
Remember that I loved you way back then
Remember
That I have blessed you time and time again

Remember when
You fell down and asked me for help
When I reached out to guide you
To lead you and order your steps

Remember no one has ever sought the Father
And found He was not there
Remember there is no burden too heavy
To be lightened by a prayer

Remember,
That just before you lost your life completely
When you couldn't muster a word,
Just cried and couldn't sleep
I heard the pain and sorrow
That was breaking your heart

Wings

Remember, I've been here for you
Right from the very start
I sent an angel in the form of man
To plant a mustard seed of faith

So, at times like these you'd remember when
And keep running to finish the race
Your rewards are waiting in heaven
At the gates where you'll enter in
When I'll look in the book and say…
Yes, my child…I remember when!

Until that time remember
That I love you unconditionally
I'm always here for you
In your deepest hour of need

Remember that no problem is too intricate
And no sorrow that you face
Is ever too deep or devastating
To be softened by God's grace!

"Take a deep breath in, feel the sun on your soul. Start fresh today, make peace your goal." **Melanie Moushigian Koulouris**

Soul Peace

Peace I leave with you, my peace I give unto you: not as the world giveth, give I unto you. Let not your heart be troubled, neither let it be afraid. John 14:27

In the still of the night as I glance at the sky
The dark while yet daunting doesn't scare me
As I lay me down to sleep
And ask you Lord my soul to keep
Peace sweet peace consumes my soul
In the still of the night, my spirit takes flight
With the moon and stars I soar to higher heights
Peace sweet peace
Keeps my mind grounded
And my feet forever landing
On good ground,
Standing in the still waters of
Peace sweet peace
What a joyful sound,
The sound of love that makes the world go 'round
The sound of peace, that lets freedom ring
Peace sweet peace
It's my song to sing!
From all that toils and troubles
What joyous relief
My soul is at peace!

Sufficient

And he said unto me, "My grace is sufficient for thee: for my strength is made perfect in weakness." Most gladly therefore will I rather glory in my infirmities, that the power of Christ may rest upon me. II Corinthians 12:9

My grace is enough; it's all you need.
We tell others His grace is sufficient
That He shall supply all of our needs
How is it then that we get caught up
In lust, power, ego trips and greed?

He gave is free will to make our own choices
It's all about "I" as we brag and boast
Like we've done something so great
Ironic the world's rotting, bound in sin and hate

Prejudice, envy and jealousy
Anger, frustration and hostility
Have captured the minds of our children
Are parked on our streets

Love don't live here anymore
The welcome sign posted on our doors
We don't show care or love for each other
We don't care to encourage our sisters and brothers
What a sad state the world is in
I can relate to how God felt
When Adam and Eve sinned
The earth is nothing like his heavenly vision

Wings

They broke his heart and we're doing the same
Yet for anyone willing to call on his name
Saving grace yet remains
Available
It's ours for the asking

Perhaps we'll soon recognize
His grace is sufficient
When we seek him with our whole heart
We shall find he really does supply all that we need
We don't need to fall prey to the world's greed.

The Man that Stands

Blessed is the man that endureth temptation: for when he is tried, he shall receive the crown of life, which the Lord hath promised to them that love him. James 1:12

Some years ago he made a vow,
Over the years at times he wondered,
"Lord, oh Lord how?"
How could he make it, how would he survive?
Courage, strength and love were buried deep inside,
Faith kept him going,
During the times he wanted to hide.
Days passed by, the years came and went,
Blessings began flowing,
And he saw it was time well spent.
Knowledge and wisdom,
Characteristics from you he sought,
More blessings flowed,
Proving his efforts were not forgot.
Trials came with tribulation and persecution too,
Yet he stood on your word,
And continued to serve you,
They laughed, they mocked,
On the church doors they put locks,
Attempting in many ways to discourage and block.
To block his forward movement,
Block his reaching the goal,
Thinking the pressure on him,
Would soon take its' toll.

Wings

Yet he stood still and he served you more and more,
Believing all the while that's what he's created for,
Today on his birthday on his faith he still stands,
With praise in his heart, he stands in service of you,
Preaching, teaching and praying just as you taught him to.
Loving the difficult, working to save the lost,
Spreading the good news of your gospel,
Sparing no cost.
Sanders White, Sr.
Your son, your student and servant,
The man that stands in your grace, dedicated and loyal,
Waiting patiently for the crown of jewels oh so royal.
The crown of a royal servant, so tried and true,
Praising and loving you daily for all that you do,
What you do for him and the rest of us too.
The man that stands in awe of your mighty power,
Growing, nurturing, and flourishing,
With every passing hour.
Grace your son dear Father,
As he continues the tasks at hand,
Bless him oh Lord for his faithfulness,
Bless him oh Lord – bless the man that stands!

"Life is not easy for any of us. But what of that? We must have perseverance and above all confidence in ourselves. We must believe that we are gifted for something and that this thing must be attained." **Marie Curie**

Today

It is of the Lord's mercies that we are not consumed, because his compassions fail not. They are new every morning: great is thy faithfulness. Lamentations 3:22-23

Today...is a new day and God's mercy is new every morning.

Yesterday is gone. Tomorrow may never come.
But...Today...you have the gift of life. Today God gave you a present...all wrapped up in the colors of the rainbow...what is this gift you may be wondering? Well in case you didn't know...it's a new opportunity to rise up...to wrap your arms around His love...to breathe in His beauty...to embrace His joy...to pursue His passion...to walk in His will...to receive His blessings!

Today...you have everything you need.
Today...you are blessed beyond measure.
Today... the joy of the Lord is your strength.
Today...the peace of God quiets your fears.
Today...the love of God silences your tears.
Today...the hand of God points the course of your direction.
Today...the Word of God answers your every question.

Today is precious...remember it is a gift. Take a little time with others, give someone else a lift. Today is the day that the Lord has made...Rejoice Today and Be Glad in it!

Michele L. Smith

What Have You Done?

And whatsoever ye do in word or deed, do all in the name of the Lord Jesus, giving thanks to God and the Father by him. Colossians 3:17

What have you done for me lately?
Have you sat quietly and patiently waited to hear from me?
Have you called someone up
To share with them what I have done for thee?
Have you stopped to appreciate the air that you breathe?
Have you walked on the sand
And relished the smell of the sea?
When heat was hot and I provided a shade tree,
Did you even think to thank me for the cool of the breeze?
Have you fallen on your knees
On behalf of another to pray and intercede?
Have you visited someone sick, depressed or lonely?
Have you been a friend to someone as I have been to thee?
Have you fed someone who had a hunger pain?
What have you done for me lately?
If none of these things you have done,
Your days have been wasted,
Your deeds done in vain.
You truly have no heart for me
If you don't care about another's pain.
So before you spend your time
Wondering and worrying about what gifts others will bring,
Remember that there so much more to life
Than mere material things.
But I have your treasures stored up for you
I am waiting
For you to recognize they are yours for the taking
Always remember what you are called to do for me.

Wings

So, I won't need to ask
What have you done for me lately?

Work in Progress

But now, O Lord, thou art our father; we are the clay, and thou our potter; and we all are the work of thy hand. Isaiah 64:8

From the moment of conception,
Until we take our first breath
From the moment of our birth,
Until the time of our death
We're taught what to do and what not to
Yet of all the lessons we learn in life
There's one that suits us best
And that is to remember
That we are merely a Work In Progress!
From the moment of salvation,
From the hour of baptism
We seek the solace of the Lord,
 In the comfort that He's risen
Risen high above the earth all power in His hands
Watching daily as we grow
Learning the laws of the land
And in our Christian walk with God
Learning love and faithfulness
Daily we must remember that we are merely a Work in
Progress!
When someone makes you angry
And another makes you cry
When things are not going quite your way
And you don't understand why
When the car breaks down and the bills are due
When you feel pretty lost
And aren't sure of what to do
Spend some time remembering His suffering

Wings

And all Jesus gave for you
Remember His sacrifice
And daily renewed forgiveness
Remember that we are merely a Work in Progress!
Beings that once were lost
And now have life renewed
Remember that He cares today
The same as when He died for you
When you feel tired and don't want to go on
Remember for you He carried the cross
And wore the crown of thorns
When you are sad and all worn out
When your life's a mess
You're full of doubt
Remember you deserve to have nothing but the best
Remember that this life
Is merely a Work in Progress!
Don't cast your eyes down on others
You must instead love your sisters and brothers
Don't let your mind be a playground for Satan
Don't spend your time being jealous and hatin'
For you must look deep within
And deal with the mess of your own sin
You must die to self and selfishness,
For you are merely a Work in Progress!
Your life is like a mold of clay
Molded by the potter's hands
Your shape is formed and strengthened
Each time you take a stand
A stand to live a Godly life
In spite of all the trials and strife
A stand to be a Christian child,
Helping someone else feel worthwhile
Your journey here is a simple one
And you must stay the course and run

Michele L. Smith

Run the race He made for you,
Saving others and giving more
More of the love He gives to you,
Pass along and the grace and awesome goodness
Never forget you are God's Work in Progress!

"I am a work in progress. Dressed in the fabric of a world unfolding.
Offering me intricate patterns of questions. Rhythms that never
come clean and strengths that you still haven't seen."
Ani DiFranco

Michele L. Smith

You Picked Me Up

*I will love thee, O Lord, my strength. The Lord is my rock, and my
fortress, and my deliverer; my God, my strength, in whom I will trust;
my buckler, and the horn of my salvation, and my high tower. He
brought me forth also into a large place, he delivered me, because he
delighted in me. Psalm 18:1-2, 19*

The day was balmy and overcast,
I'd had fun all day and it was time to go at last.
I had no idea the havoc satan was trying to wreak,
Yet you reached down and caused death to cease.
As my body fell and rolled on the ground,
I didn't utter a word, couldn't make a sound.
Losing consciousness and all touch with reality,
You reached down and sustained life in me.
A fractured skull and severely bruised brain,
Literally my body ached and burned with pain.
The pain was so awful I just wanted to sleep,
But sleep would not come,
Because my classmates were so busy,
They wouldn't stop talking, laughing or teasing.
I had no understanding, not the slightest clue,
That you were using them to help me,
Because you had work for me to do.
The doctors said had I gone to sleep,
I would have died,
When those words I heard,
I broke down and cried.
I had no revelation,
You'd already set the call on my life,
That your assignment to me was my life to write.
To learn your will, do your work,
Run the Christian race,

54

Wings

To share my story, your love,
Forgiveness and grace.
To lift and encourage those who've lost hope,
To aid in deliverance from lust, alcohol and dope,
The demons which I myself would face,
The tools to use to help others grow in faith.
You reached down in your love for me,
To save my soul and set me free.
You lifted me away from an early death,
You gave me a second chance to pass the love test.
To share the love that you daily give,
With everyone I encounter each day that I live.
You looked down and picked me up,
For such a time as this,
Day after day you have filled my cup,
Poured into my life joy and happiness.
Blessings flow abundantly,
Health, wealth, prosperity and peace,
Love, encouragement, never ending support,
Thank you, my Lord!
I'm so thankful God
That You Picked Me Up!

Michele L. Smith

Uncertain Love

Keep your eyes open, hold tight to your convictions, give it all you've got, be resolute, and love without stopping.
I Corinthians 16:13-14 (The Message)

Questions burn like the raging wind
Rolling across our minds over and over again
What happened we ask to us way back then
How we ask ourselves
Did our love grown uncertain?
We were young
We suppose and lacked understanding
Even though we had pledged a love everlasting
Our feelings raw and real,
Our intentions true and pure
Yet doubt crept in and we became unsure
Fear and insecurity clouded our vision
Hearts torn to pieces, our oneness was broken
Runaway emotions caused our division
Sweet innocence soured
As our love turned uncertain
We questioned ourselves then just like we do now
Wondering why, when and yes, even how
How would we make it we tried to comprehend
Battling the forces that turned our love uncertain
Time passed on as it waits for no one
New paths were forged, new stepping stones
We boxed and packed away portions of our hearts
Life compelled us to get up and make a fresh start
Love would come again in new shapes and faces
As we attempted to bury the old love traces
But a threefold chord can never be broken

Wings

Even when love is secret and unspoken
Purpose has joined our paths once again
That we might heal, forgive and erase the pain
You're a part of me and me a part of you
Today we know it to be sincere and true
It's a new season, it's a new day
No longer need we wonder why we feel this way
No longer do we wonder
No longer do we question
For what we once thought eluded us
Is no longer an illusion
I realize now it is a divine connection
Love
True Love
God given love
Not a love uncertain
Love that is patient
Love that is kind
God given love for the rest of our lives
I thank God for you and the love that we share
Love deeply rooted and I believe rare
Thank you for loving me as no one else has
Just as much today as in the days past
For looking beyond my flaws and loving me for me
For being my friend completely and unconditionally.

SOAR

"Jesus said unto him, If thou canst believe, all things are possible to him that believeth." Mark 9:23

Sometimes in this life we box ourselves in
Forgetting that God gave us power and dominion
Dominion to conquer
Power to create, prosper and thrive
We self-impose limits that hinder our progress
Delaying or sabotaging our own success
We say the sky is the limit
Yet we fail to reach outside the four walls of our existence
We don't fail because we are afraid
We fail because we lack faith
The eagle rises above the storm
He enjoys the solace of flying alone
The eagle doesn't settle for mediocre
He knows he was created to soar
Much can be learned from the eagle
You cease to learn if you're unteachable
Don't let society wrap you up like stale bread
Greatness is on the inside of you
Unleash the power within
Free your mind
Release the ties that bind
Learn to unleash your vision
Execute your potential
Achieve your dreams
Plan your happiness
Life is sweet when you LEAP
Dare to be all you were created to be
Spread your wings and SOAR!

"One can never consent to creep when one feels an impulse to soar."

Helen Keller

If and When

But if any of you lacks wisdom, let him ask of God, who gives to all generously and without reproach, and it will be given to him. But he must ask in faith without any doubting, for the one who doubts is like the surf of the sea, driven and tossed by the wind. For that man ought not to expect that he will receive anything from the Lord,
James 1:5-7 (NASB)

Stuck between if and when
Wondering if you'll trust and love again
Questioning why you gave so much power to him
Questioning why you abandoned all your friends
True love was what thought you had
Now you're depressed, lonely and sad
Frustrated, stressed and plenty mad
You want to blame him for all your pain
Deep down inside you feel completely ashamed
Of the fact that you let things go as you did
All the secrets, skeletons and lies that you hid
But it's alright...Wake up girl, smell the coffee
There's no need to be driving yourself crazy
Time keeps on ticking, life goes on
The sun always shines just after the storm
Pick yourself up, get out of that bed
Take a Calgon bath, clear your head
Release the tears, go ahead let 'em flow
Let go of it all so you are troubled no more
Be encouraged girl, stand on your faith
Hold your head up high; put a smile on your face
Rejoice in the Lord, give God some praise
Because life is not over it's only just begun
Get ready, get set, you've got a race to run
You've been looking for love

In all the wrong places
Love is not found in the handsome men's faces
Love is in the heart genuine and pure
One thing I know and of this I am sure
God loved you then, loves you now and He always will
You just need to step back, chill and be still
Be still and know that He IS God
Seek the Lord first and his righteousness
And never again will you cry
Over a man and his mess
Stuck between If and When
Being tossed to and fro in a spinning whirlwind
Is only a mindset created by sin
It's time to let go girl
Let go and Let God
Surrender your mind, body and soul
Let God and Let God have complete control
You don't need a man to live and be free
In God you have all power and divine authority
You're His queen – You are the one
You are the one chosen for such a time as this
Hand-picked to bring others out of the abyss
You are the anointed and empowered
Empowered to rise and shine in this hour
You are the one who is the apple of God's eyes
You are the one destined to save lives
You are the one made in His image
Filled with His beauty – endowed with His love
Knitted to him like a hand in the glove
You are the one that deserves nothing less
Than the blessings inside Daddy's treasure chest
God says
My precious daughter
Stuck between If and When is not a place
Where I ever want you to dwell again

Michele L. Smith

So don't stand stuck between If and When
But sing your song
Do your dance
Trust me I'm coming strong on your behalf
Be encouraged
Rise Up
Stand
Be Empowered

Stand Still

Hearken unto this, O Job: stand still, and consider the wondrous works of God. Job 37:14

Stand still,
And consider the wondrous works of God
Harness the power of God's unfailing love
Hear God speak in the hummingbird's song
Watch the glory of God's grace in the flying dove
Stand still,
Breathe in the beauty of all God's creation
Give honor to the Lord for the gift of salvation
Relax sometimes and just relish the moment
Bask in the preciousness of all that's heaven sent
Stand still,
And recognize that all God made is good
Behold the duty to walk in His love, if you would
Transcend the journey of abundant joy each day
Grasp hold of the bountiful blessings
Lining the path of life's highway
Stand still,
Feel the freshness of the dew in the morning
Cast your eye on the sunset over the land glowing
Inhale the fragrance of the multitude of flowers
Listen to the ocean waters roar of God's power
In the busyness of life
Take some time to just…Stand Still
Stand still,
And consider the wondrous works of God.

Limitless

*For my thoughts are not your thoughts, neither are your ways my
ways, saith the Lord.
For as the heavens are higher than the earth, so are my ways higher
than your ways, and my thoughts than your thoughts.*
Isaiah 55:8-9

Limitation by association
Disrupts my mental relaxation
I have too much to do
No time to be wasting
Frustration results from the hesitation
Indecision is a distraction
Fluctuating emotions
Interrupt the flow of my imagination
Your perception of my ability
Reflects your own insecurity
Don't box me in because of your fears
I'm made perfect in my weakness
Through the hand of the Father
With small minds and thoughts
I can't be bothered
I am limitless
Fulfilling purpose and destiny
Limitless…that's me

Wings

"Limitations live only in our minds. But if we use our imaginations, our possibilities become limitless." **Jamie Paolinetti**

Reflection

As in water face reflects face, So a man's heart reveals the man.
Proverbs 27:19 (NKJV)

Reflection is designed as mental concentration,
A Thought or opinion resulting from careful consideration.
When you close your eyes and meditate on the goodness of
God,
What awesome thoughts must come to mind
For all that He has done!
Your time of reflection is to be a testimony,
The witness of the glory that results when you share your story.
Reflections bring about the "I remember when,"
And should bear witness of how
God's kept you time and time again.
Remember,
When your body pained, hurt and ached
How He healed you while you only had mustard seed faith.
Remember,
The times when you had not a dime
How He provided what was needed just in the nick of time.
Remember,
The times you were lost and so afraid?
How He guided you safely,
Whispering "My child be ye not dismayed."
Remember,
The times you hurt someone and didn't apologize,
God never turned His back on you, nor did He criticize.
Remember,
Before all these things, before you were even born,
How the world even way back then was graven and forlorn
Yet God was determined that your life would be special

Wings

That you would be filled with love, you would be His treasure
All the while He planned for you while you did your own thing
Knowing you may reject Him, He remained forgiving.
God never faltered or drew back from His plans,
He continued to keep you covered in the power of His hands.
It's time to step back now and do some serious reflecting,
Then witness boldly to others of God's love and longsuffering.
Remember,
That your time of reflection is not meant just for you,
But meant to encourage others
To save them from what you went through.
Your time of reflection,
Should be one of sincere thanks and praise,
It should constantly bless you,
Ad help you grow in faith.
Now is the time for a season of reflection
On the AWESOME greatness of God
And His never-ending affection!

A Mother's Heartache

And blessed is she that believed: for there shall be a performance of those things which were told her from the Lord. Luke 1:45

Twenty-three years ago he lay growing in the womb
An anxious mother to be knew that he'd be born soon
Excited and yet nervous about mothering a son
With the first glimpse of his face her heart was son
Joy and happiness grew with him each day
She grew to love him more than she could say
So small and sweet her adorable little boy
For hours she'd sit and watch him play with his toys
The radiance in his smile warmed her heart
A heart burning of a mother's love right from the start
Years passed on and her little boy grew
No longer was he the son his mother thought she knew
Hidden secrets, broken promises, excuses and lies
For the mother and son such became a way of life
Sadness, tears, frustration and pain
All rolled up into a mother's heartache
She questioned, pondered and wondered why
Her son would walk the path of misery and strife
Couldn't he see the mistakes she had made?
Didn't he know life wasn't supposed to be this way?
Bright and intelligent, filled with potential
Why couldn't he see he was destined to be influential?
Why couldn't he see what a difference he could make?
Time passed on and so continued a mother's heartache
She prayed and cried, she moaned and groaned
'Til one day God told her you must leave him alone
He was my son before he was yours
I gave him to you as a gift

Wings

I allowed you to care for him
And sometimes you slipped
You've prayed to me and I heard your cry
Yet you keep asking me, "Why God why?"
The reason is that you must leave him with me
Only he and I can work it out so that he is free
Free from the guilt, the hurt and the shame
Free from the pains of feeling betrayed
Free from those things that have him in bondage
Free from the burdens and excess baggage
He is my son and I love him so much
All he needs is to ask for my touch
Until that time you need cry no more
Just trust me like you never have before
Forgive yourself as I have forgiven you
Let me be God and do what I do
The day soon shall come when you will give me praise
For no longer will you suffer a mother's heartache!

Michele L. Smith

Sweet Mama

God is in the midst of her; she shall not be moved: God shall help her, and that right early. Psalm 46:5

For all you do and all you've done
Whether it be for your daughters or your sons
Your work and labor has not been in vain
God knows your heart and He feels your pain.
He knows about the times you wept and cried
About every time the kids rebelled and fed you lies
He knows about the struggles you've been through
About the nights you laid awake
Wondering what you should do
He remembers the assignment he placed on your life
He knows you might be a mother and never a wife
He knows your hearts desires and your daily woes
He remembers how you smiled
When counting the fingers and toes
The children may never seem to care
But turn your back on them you wouldn't dare
No matter what they say or do
You hold fast and keep giving love so true
The mother's love that compares to no other
The love only you and a child can share with each other
A bond that is as strong as iron and steel
A love learned from God that's solid and real
One thing you must always remember
Each year from January through December
That no matter the day or even the weather
You are a precious jewel, a sweet royal treasure
Though the work is often tiring
And the "thank-you's" seem few

Wings

God's watching you Mama and He appreciates you
He will continue to provide strength for the journey
Trust in Him and believe He doesn't want you to worry
He has your back each and every step of the way
Not just when the world celebrates Mother's Day
So be encouraged Mama whether you are young or old
Remember that in you God unfolds the rose
We celebrate sweet mama
Knowing that God will keep you
Even in the family folk's drama
He folds down the petals of the days of your lives
Honoring you for serving amidst the trials and strife
Your gentle beauty and sweet spirit are praise to Him
Let go and let God deposit peace within
Your soul and your heart deserve divine protection
Protection made possible through a heavenly connection
Be encouraged, don't fret, smile, relax and ENJOY
Your cup is soon to be running over with blessings galore
Slow down and rest your head on the heart of God
Let His abundance flow as it never has before
Everything you need the rest of this year
Is already provided, it's settled and secure!
Be Encouraged Sweet Mama.

Michele L. Smith

"The starts may fall, but God's promises will stand and be fulfilled."

J.I. Packer

Godsister

Two are better than one; because they have a good reward for their labour. For if they fall, the one will lift up his fellow: but woe to him that is alone when he falleth; for he hath not another to help him up. Again, if two lie together, then they have heat: but how can one be warm alone? And if one prevail against him, two shall withstand him; and a threefold cord is not quickly broken. Ecclesiastes 4:9-12

As we remain sisters through the years
We may smile, laugh and shed some tears
We may have harsh words and pull our hair
But to a sister's love none can compare
For it's a sacred bond we were created to share
Always my sister know that I care
I care for you and the things you go through
I'm here when you need me
And I know you'll be there for me too
Our times together may be few
But my sister I will always love and cherish you
A sister loves in ways that are unspoken
God says our bond must never be broken
And we must stay in fellowship
According to His Word
You are my God-give, God-appointed sister
This we cannot deny
No matter how we may think or feel
At any given time
You are a part of me and me a part of you
It's according to our Father's plan
That together in unity and sisterhood we stand
I pray your Peace, Joy, Love and Happiness
I pray for Sisterhood
Free of envy, jealousy and selfishness

Michele L. Smith

Encouragement and support
To each other we must give
This is the command of the Father
For each day that we live
You are beautiful, royal gentle and kind
A woman of commitment, character and integrity
I humbly myself in honor of you as my sister
Now and in eternity!

Women of Integrity

Better the poor whose walk is blameless than the rich whose ways are perverse. Proverbs 28:6 (NIV)

Wonderfully and beautifully He made you and me,
Destined to be Women of Integrity.
Made from the rib of man,
Molded like clay in the potter's hands.

Filled with compassion, compelled to stand,
To stand and live a godly life,
To help other women learn they are worthwhile,
Graced to carry and bare the gift of life.

To serve as daughters, sisters, mothers and wives,
Triumphant through trials, tribulation and strife,
Trusting the Lord to guide our path,
Thankful that He saved us from our wretched past.

Transformed through forgiveness into priceless treasures,
Excited to send up praises for the Father's pleasure,
Diligent servants on the battlefield of faith,
Prayer warriors interceding on behalf of the saints.

Walking the streets in Jesus' name,
God's love we proclaim,
Never casting judgment or looking down on others,
Embracing and loving our sisters and brothers.

Praying, fasting, studying the word,
Walking daily with God,
Learning love and steadfastness,

Michele L. Smith

Always remembering we are His Work In Progress.

Staying steady on the course for our journey's a simple one,
To stand, and stand and stand ever more,
To pass along to other God's grace and goodness,
Giving much thanks for how greatly we are blessed.

An integral part of one big family,
Recognizing each member is a necessity,
Working together for the common good,
That God's word be known and fully understood.

To impart knowledge and revelation,
To share information, provide education,
To shelter the weak from the storm,
To encourage the young child living without a mom.

To love and to give love it's our job you must know,
To love in spirit and truth…not just for show,
Spend some time remembering His ultimate love for you,
Because once you were lost and without a clue.

Yet He came in the flesh and shed his precious blood,
For you to have life…life renewed.
Individually and collectively,
We are Women of Integrity.

Individually and collectively, we've got some work to do.
I'm ready and God's asking are you ready too?
If so then Stand in the Spirit of Unity.
Stand and be the most awesome woman that you can be.
Go forth in character…God's Women of Integrity!

Time is Winding Up

He hath made everything beautiful in its time. Ecclesiastes 3:11

Time is winding up; it's a new season, a new day.
Time for the children of God to make a change,
The time for change is here and now,
Trust God and don't question why or how.
Time is winding up, desperation's setting in,
You can't turn back,
Even when your mind says give up and give in.
Just start making a change,
In the way you spend your time.
There are precious few seconds,
Standing between you and a lost soul's life.
Time is winding up,
God says there's no need to look back,
Follow Him and you'll never again get off track.
The sanctuary is full of angels,
Waiting to welcome you in,
Time is winding up,
'Til Jesus is with us again.
God is waiting patiently,
For us to open our eyes and see,
That our best time will be that spent in ETERNITY!

Michele L. Smith

"Time is free, but it's priceless. You can't own it, but you can use it. You can't keep, but you can spend it. Once you've lost it you can never get it back." **Harvey Mackay**

The Knots Prayer

Dear God :

Please untie the knots that are in my mind ,
my heart my life.

Remove the have nots ,
the can nots and the do nots
that I have in my mind

Erase all the will nots ,
might nots
that may find a home in my heart .

Release me from the could nots
would nots
that obstruct my life .

And most of all
Dear God ;
I ask that you remove from my mind ,
my heart and my life
all the 'am nots'
that I have allowed to hold me back ,
especially the thought,
that I am not good enough

Author Known to God

When Darkness Falls

"Let us hold tightly without wavering to the hope we affirm, for God can be trusted to keep His promise." Hebrews 10:23 (NIV)

Sometimes no matter how strong your faith
Or how hard and long you pray
Seeds of distraction grow and take root
Darkness fills your thoughts clouding your day
Doubt creeps in like a thief in the night
Stealing your hope
Shattering your heart like a broken glass
Weariness sets in, you're ready to give up the fight
Your mind is spinning
Faster than the horse on the carousel
You can't turn off the switch
Every muscle in your body seems to twitch
Frustration
Disappointment
Anger
Hurt
Emotions are holding you hostage
You slip into despair
Convinced God is not there and no one cares
Believing the darkness will never dissipate
You close your eyes hoping for some relief
Jesus whispers, "I'm here, right here don't fear"
The darkest hour is just before dawn."
In the closet of your mind you see a ray of light
It seems galaxies away
"Hold on," Jesus says
"Hold on to me when darkness falls
Hold on to me as the tears fall down your face

Wings

Hold on when it seems like your prayers have blown away
Weeping may endure for the night
But joy comes in the morning
Hold on to me when darkness falls
Be assured that you have all you need
I'll never leave you nor forsake you
Rest in my arms, be at peace
Hold on to me when darkness falls."

Unstoppable

Be of good courage, and He shall strengthen your heart, all ye that hope in the Lord. Psalm 31:24

The call is urgent, the time is now
Gifts have been given
A ministry born
To meet the needs of those who are lost
Reaching out to edify, encourage, uplift
To stand in the gap no matter the cost
The stories keep coming
They're crying out for help
They're lost they know
Searching to understand why
The march is on to save their lives
Help them to stand strong and fight
Assure them they are not alone
That in Christ there is hope
Together we must help each other cope
God gave the vision
To inspire the people and break through doubt
From young and old, black brown & white,
All shapes and sizes, all walks of life
Revealing the hurts, the pain and the strife
They come one by one,
Sometimes they come in pairs
They laugh, they cry, they talk, they share
Our job is to reassure them that God is always there
From fear, depression and anxiety
Through the years we've seen it all,
Anger, rebellion and selfishness
Satan's stumbling blocks out to make them fall

Wings

From baby mama drama to death and divorce
Through the years I've seen it all
Every negative force
No matter what the circumstances or the obstacles
I've got to help them keep on trekking
Towards the streets of gold
At one time or another I've been there
By God's grace I made it through
Now I must show others they can make it too
Searching for answers, for hope and for love
Teach them to pull strength from our Father above
In Him nothing is impossible
Assure them in Christ they are unstoppable.

Michele L. Smith

"The only limits you have are the limits you believe." **Wayne Dyer**

Life Bouquet

These things have I spoken unto you, that my joy might remain in you, and that your joy might be full. John 15:11

Talking with a sister friend about her relationship
She was getting stuck between if and when
She'd been hurt and caused some pain
Determined not to go down that road again
She yearned for happiness
I understood her confusion
"God," I said, "Tell me what to do."

As we talked, God began to show me a bouquet of flowers: Life, love and relationships are likened unto a bouquet of flowers. Initially, some buds are in full bloom, some are still closed. As the connection develops, the petals unfold until such time as the whole bouquet is in full bloom. Time marches on, life happens and change takes place. Petals begin to wilt (relationships wither). Eventually your life flowers die – physically or emotionally. You may press some petals in your memory book, or just empty the vase. You don't say to the flowers: "Why did you die?" or "I'm devastated because you left me," because you know it's the natural progression of the flower's life cycle. You simply say goodbye to the flowers and release them.

Consider making this practical application to your life: Enjoy the Beauty of it as it is while it is and when it's gone Be Thankful that you had it while it was what it was rather than being angry or hurt that it is no more.

Michele L. Smith

Live like there's no tomorrow. Laugh every day. Love like you've never been hurt. Appreciate each flower in your life's bouquet for the love, joy and beauty they add to your existence. Bask in the Beauty of your Life's Bouquet.

Live Your Life Royally

But you are a chosen people, a royal priesthood, a holy nation, God's special possession, that you may declare the praises of him who called you out of darkness into his wonderful light.
I Peter 2:9

You are a royal priesthood
A peculiar nation
Created in the image of God
With power and dominion
His love is your power
His joy is your strength
Dare to be your own kind of beautiful
Don't be afraid to pursue your dreams
Life has a way of throwing curve balls
Just keep believing and giving your all
Step out in faith
Give it all you've got
With God on your side you can't be stopped
You are precious in His sight
Deserving of His best
Give it all you've got
Let God handle the rest
You are unique, amazing and so much more
Spread your wings this day and soar
Go ahead sons and daughters of the King
Live Your Life Royally!

"May all your hopes, dreams and prayers be carried on the wings of eagles, high into the air and there to fall softly, upon the ears of the great spirit." **William Purcell**

Bible Reading Plan

Reading the referenced passage each day, you will read the entire Bible in one year. Start reading today, there is no better time than the present. Schedule a specific time each day for your personal reading. Pray when you begin. Ask the Holy Spirit for wisdom and understanding. Keep track of your reading and enjoy your journey through the Word of God.

Date	Passage	Completed
1	Genesis 1-4	
2	Genesis 5-8	
3	Genesis 9-12	
4	Genesis 13-17	
5	Genesis 18-20	
6	Genesis 21-23	
7	Genesis 24-25	
8	Genesis 26-28	
9	Genesis 29-31	
10	Genesis 32-35	
11	Genesis 36-38	
12	Genesis 39-41	
13	Genesis 42-43	
14	Genesis 44-46	

15	Genesis 47-50	
16	Exodus 1-4	
17	Exodus 5-7	
18	Exodus 8-10	
19	Exodus 11-13	
20	Exodus 14-16	
21	Exodus 17-20	
22	Exodus 21-23	
23	Exodus 24-27	
24	Exodus 28-30	
25	Exodus 31-34	
26	Exodus 35-37	
27	Exodus 38-40	
28	Leviticus 1-4	
29	Leviticus 5-7	
30	Leviticus 8-10	
31	Leviticus 11-13	
32	Leviticus 14-15	
33	Leviticus 16-18	
34	Leviticus 19-21	
35	Leviticus 22-23	
36	Leviticus 24-25	
37	Leviticus 26-27	

38	Numbers 1-2	
39	Numbers 3-4	
40	Numbers 5-6	
41	Numbers 7	
42	Numbers 8-10	
43	Numbers 11-13	
44	Numbers 14-15	
45	Numbers 16-18	
46	Numbers 19-21	
47	Numbers 22-24	
48	Numbers 25-26	
49	Numbers 27-29	
50	Numbers 30-32	
51	Numbers 33-36	
52	Deuteronomy 1-2	
53	Deuteronomy 3-4	
54	Deuteronomy 5-8	
55	Deuteronomy 9-11	
56	Deuteronomy 12-15	
57	Deuteronomy16-19	
58	Deuteronomy 20-22	
59	Deuteronomy 23-25	
60	Deuteronomy 26-27	

Michele L. Smith

61	Deuteronomy 28-29	
62	Deuteronomy 30-32	
63	Deuteronomy 33-34	
64	Joshua 1-4	
65	Joshua 5-7	
66	Joshua 8-10	
67	Joshua 11-13	
68	Joshua 14-17	
69	Joshua 18-20	
70	Joshua 21-22	
71	Joshua 23-24	
72	Judges 1-3	
73	Judges 4-5	
74	Judges 6-8	
75	Judges 9-10	
76	Judges 11-13	
77	Judges 14-16	
78	Judges 17-19	
79	Judges 20-21	
80	Ruth 1-4	
81	I Samuel 1-3	
82	I Samuel 4-7	
83	I Samuel 8-12	

84	I Samuel 13-14	
85	I Samuel 15-16	
86	I Samuel 17-18	
87	I Samuel19-21	
88	I Samuel 22-24	
89	I Samuel 25-27	
90	I Samuel 28-31	
91	II Samuel 1-3	
92	II Samuel 4-7	
93	II Samuel 8-11	
94	II Samuel 12-13	
95	II Samuel 14-16	
96	II Samuel 17-19	
97	II Samuel 20-22	
98	II Samuel 23-24	
99	I Kings 1-2	
100	I Kings 3-5	
101	I Kings 6-7	
102	I Kings 8-9	
103	I Kings 10-12	
104	I Kings 13-15	
105	I Kings 16-18	
106	I Kings 19-20	

107	I Kings 21-22	
108	II Kings 1-3	
109	II Kings 4-5	
110	II Kings 6-8	
111	II Kings9-10	
112	II Kings 11-13	
113	II Kings 14-16	
114	II Kings 17-18	
115	II Kings 19-21	
116	II Kings 22-23	
117	II Kings 24-25	
118	I Chronicles 1-2	
119	I Chronicles 3-4	
120	I Chronicles 5-6	
121	I Chronicles 7-9	
122	I Chronicles 10-12	
123	I Chronicles 13-16	
124	I Chronicles 17-19	
125	I Chronicles 20-23	
126	I Chronicles 24-26	
127	I Chronicle 27-29	
128	II Chronicles 1-4	
129	II Chronicles 5-7	

130	II Chronicles 8-11	
131	II Chronicles 12-16	
132	II Chronicles 17-20	
133	II Chronicles 21-24	
134	II Chronicles 25-28	
135	II Chronicles 29-31	
136	II Chronicles 32-34	
137	II Chronicles 35-36	
138	Ezra 1-4	
139	Ezra 5-7	
140	Ezra 8-10	
141	Nehemiah 1-3	
142	Nehemiah 4-7	
143	Nehemiah 8-10	
144	Nehemiah 11-13	
145	Esther 1-5	
146	Esther 6-10	
147	Job 1-4	
148	Job 5-8	
149	Job 9-12	
150	Job 13-16	
151	Job 17-20	
152	Job 21-24	

153	Job 25-30	
154	Job 31-34	
155	Job 35-38	
156	Jo 39-42	
157	Psalms 1-8	
158	Psalms 9-17	
159	Psalms 18-21	
160	Psalms 22-27	
161	Psalms 28-33	
162	Psalms 34-37	
163	Psalms 38-42	
164	Psalms 43-49	
165	Psalms 50-55	
166	Psalms 56-61	
167	Psalms 62-68	
168	Psalms 69-72	
169	Psalms 73-77	
170	Psalms 78-80	
171	Psalms 81-88	
172	Psalms 89-94	
173	Psalms 95-103	
174	Psalms 104-106	
175	Psalms 107-111	

176	Psalms 112-118	
177	Psalms 119	
178	Psalms 120-133	
179	Psalms 134-140	
180	Psalms 141-150	
181	Proverbs 1-3	
182	Proverbs 4-7	
183	Proverbs 8-11	
184	Proverbs 12-14	
185	Proverbs 15-17	
186	Proverbs 18-20	
187	Proverbs 21-23	
188	Proverbs 24-26	
189	Proverbs 27-29	
190	Proverbs 30-31	
191	Ecclesiastes 1-4	
192	Ecclesiastes 5-8	
193	Ecclesiastes 9-12	
194	Song of Solomon 1-4	
195	Song of Solomon 5-8	
196	Isaiah 1-3	
197	Isaiah 4-8	
198	Isaiah 9-11	

199	Isaiah 12-14	
200	Isaiah 15-19	
201	Isaiah 20-24	
202	Isaiah 25-28	
203	Isaiah 29-31	
204	Isaiah 32-34	
205	Isaiah 35-37	
206	Isaiah 38-40	
207	Isaiah 41-43	
208	Isaiah 44-46	
209	Isaiah 47-49	
210	Isaiah 50-52	
211	Isaiah 53-56	
212	Isaiah 57-59	
213	Isaiah 60-63	
214	Isaiah 64-66	
215	Jeremiah 1-3	
216	Jeremiah 4-5	
217	Jeremiah 6-8	
218	Jeremiah 9-11	
219	Jeremiah 12-14	
220	Jeremiah 15-17	
221	Jeremiah 18-21	

222	Jeremiah 22-24	
223	Jeremiah 25-27	
224	Jeremiah 28-30	
225	Jeremiah 31-32	
226	Jeremiah 33-36	
227	Jeremiah 37-39	
228	Jeremiah 40-43	
229	Jeremiah 44-46	
230	Jeremiah 47-48	
231	Jeremiah 49	
232	Jeremiah 50	
233	Jeremiah 51-52	
234	Lamentations 1-2	
235	Lamentations 3-5	
236	Ezekiel 1-4	
237	Ezekiel 5-8	
238	Ezekiel 9-12	
239	Ezekiel 13-15	
240	Ezekiel 16-17	
241	Ezekiel 18-20	
242	Ezekiel 21-22	
243	Ezekiel 23-24	
244	Ezekiel 25-27	

Michele L. Smith

245	28-30	
246	31-32	
247	33-35	
248	36-38	
249	39-40	
250	41-43	
251	44-46	
252	47-48	
253	Daniel 1-3	
254	4-5	
255	6-8	
256	9-12	
257	Hosea 1-4	
258	Hosea 5-9	
259	Hosea 10-14	
260	Joel 1-3	
261	Amos 1-4	
262	Amos 5-9	
263	Obadiah 1	
264	Jonah 1-4	
265	Micah 1-4	
266	Micah 5-7	
267	Nahum 1-3	

268	Habakkuk 1-3	
269	Zephaniah 1-3	
270	Haggai 1-2	
271	Zechariah 1-5	
272	6-10	
273	11-14	
274	Malachi 1-4	
275	Matthew 1-4	
276	5-6	
277	7-9	
278	10-11	
279	12-13	
280	14-17	
281	18-20	
282	21-22	
283	23-24	
284	25-26	
285	27-28	
286	Mark 1-3	
287	4-5	
288	6-7	
289	8-9	
290	10-11	

291	12-13	
292	14	
293	15-16	
294	Luke 1-2	
295	3-4	
296	5-6	
297	7-8	
298	9-10	
299	11-12	
300	13-15	
301	16-18	
302	19-20	
303	21-22	
304	23-24	
305	John 1-2	
306	3-4	
307	5-6	
308	7-8	
309	9-10	
310	11-12	
311	13-15	
312	16-17	
313	John 18-19	

314	John 20-21	
315	Acts 1-3	
316	Acts 4-5	
317	Acts 6-7	
318	Acts 8-9	
319	Acts 10-11	
320	Acts 12-13	
321	Acts 14-15	
322	Acts 16-17	
323	Acts 18-19	
324	Acts 20-21	
325	Acts 22-23	
326	Acts 24-26	
327	Acts 27-28	
328	Romans 1-3	
329	Romans 4-7	
330	Romans 8-10	
331	Romans 11-14	
332	Romans 15-16	
333	I Corinthians 1-4	
334	I Corinthians 5-9	
335	I Corinthians 10-13	
336	I Corinthians 14-16	

337	II Corinthians 1-4	
338	II Corinthians 5-9	
339	II Corinthians 10-13	
340	Galatians 1-3	
341	Galatians 4-6	
342	Ephesians 1-3	
343	Ephesians 4-6	
344	Philippians 1-4	
345	Colossians 1-4	
346	I Thessalonians 1-5	
347	II Thessalonians 1-3	
348	I Timothy 1-6	
349	II Timothy 1-4	
350	Philemon 1; Titus 1-3	
351	Hebrews 1-4	
352	Hebrews 5-8	
353	Hebrews 9-10	
354	Hebrews 11-13	
355	James 1-5	
356	I Peter 1-5; 2 Peter 1-3	
357	I John 1-5	
358	2 John 1; 3 John 1; Jude 1	
359	Revelation 1-3	

360	Revelation 4-7	
361	Revelation 8-11	
362	Revelation 12-14	
363	Revelation 15-17	
364	Revelation 18-19	
365	Revelation 20-22	

Notes:

I Am Affirmations

"And you will know the truth, and the truth will make you free." John 8:32. There are a great many Biblical truths that reveal who God made you to be. People say, *"You are what you eat."* Truth is, you are what you speak. As a man thinketh, so is he. Following are some I AM Affirmations. This is not meant to be a total list of all the Bible says that you are. Read them daily. Confess them out loud. Add to the list or create your own. Speak your I Am into existence. Speak those things that be not as though they were. Manifest Your I Am to Live Your Life Royally.

I Am a Believer (2 Corinthians 4:4).

I Am fearfully and wonderfully made (Psalm 139:14).

I Am in His perfect peace (Isaiah 26:3).

I Am more than a conqueror (Romans 8:37).

I Am a New Creation (2 Corinthians 5:17).

I Am able to do all things through Christ Jesus (Philippians 4:13).

I Am God's child (1 Peter 1:23).

I Am God's workmanship (Ephesians 2:10).

I Am a doer of the Word (James 1:22,25).

I Am a joint-heir with Christ (Romans 8:17).

I Am a royal priesthood, a holy nation (1 Peter 2:9).

I Am Holy and without blame (Ephesians 1:4; 1 Peter 1:16).

I Am the righteousness of God in Jesus Christ
(2 Corinthians 5:21).

I Am the temple of the Holy Spirit; (1 Corinthians 6:19).

I Am the head and not the tail; I am above only and not beneath
(Deuteronomy 28:13).

I Am the light of the world (Matthew 5:14).

I Am the salt of the earth (Matthew 5:13).

I Am His elect, (Romans 8:33; Colossians 3:12).

I Am forgiven (Ephesians 1:7).

I Am redeemed (Deuteronomy 28:15-68; Galatians 3:13).

I Am firmly rooted, built up, established in my faith
(Colossians 2:7).

I Am Healed by Jesus' stripes (Isaiah 53:5).

I Am loved (Romans 1:7; 1 Thessalonians 1:4).

I Am Victorious (Philippians 3:14).

I Am Fearless (2 Timothy 1:7).

References

www.brainyquote.com

www.christianity.com

www.livin3.com

www.boardofwisdom.com

www.biblegateway.com

The following versions of The Holy Bible were used and cited within the pages of this book.

King James Version (KJV)
The Holy Bible KJV is public domain in the United States.

New International Version (NIV)
Holy Bible, New International Version®, NIV® Copyright ©1973, 1978, 1984, 2011 by Biblica, Inc.® Used by permission. All rights reserved worldwide.

English Standard Version (ESV)
The ESV® Bible (The Holy Bible, English Standard Version®). ESV® Permanent Text Edition® (2016). Copyright © 2001 by Crossway, a publishing ministry of Good News Publishers. The ESV® text has been reproduced in cooperation with and by permission of Good News Publishers. Unauthorized reproduction of this publication is prohibited. All rights reserved.

The Message
"Scripture taken from The Message. Copyright © 1993, 1994, 1995, 1996, 2000, 2001, 2002. Used by permission of NavPress Publishing Group."

Royal Words to Guide Your Day

"Empowering people to effect change one nugget, one heart, one life at a time"

Inspirational Books, Poetry and Gifts for All Occasions. Professional writing services also available.

Let us help you give personal keepsake gifts.
Birthdays
Weddings
Anniversaries
Family Reunion
Graduation
Baptism
Ordination
Corporate Events
And more…

Place your orders securely online at www.royalwordpublications.com

12 Page Preview

Wings

Love and Faith Coloring Book

About the Author

Michele has been writing since she was a young girl. The poems and inspirations contained in Wings are the result of her life experience and continuing desire to encourage others. She is dedicated to empowering and edifying women, men and young people to discover their purpose, operate in their gifts and fulfill their destiny. Her writing has opened the door for her to express her love to those who are hurting.

Michele is dedicated to empowering and edifying others. In her capacity as a Certified Life Coach, she is co-founder of iCelebrateHER, a women's foundation whose mission is to assist women of all ages grown and prosper in every area of their lives: personally, professionally, spiritually, financially and emotionally. She is the owner of Royal Word Publications, a publishing and consulting company. She utilizes all available platforms to teach classes and moderates workshops in self-help, business start-up, professional writing and publishing.

Michele has penned numerous poems and authored two books: Precious Nuggets: Poems to Encourage the Heart and Royal Words to Guide Your Day: 30 Days of Devotion and Transformation. She is actively engaged with a number of clients preparing their manuscripts for publication and finalizing her autobiography. She donates all proceeds from her first book and a portion of sales from her other works to fund scholarships, provide school supplies and aid to domestic violence victims. To learn more about Michele and her upcoming projects visit her website: www.royalwordpublications.com.

www.ingramcontent.com/pod-product-compliance
Lightning Source LLC
LaVergne TN
LVHW021512080426
835509LV00018B/2487